THE GREAT MYOPIA

AN EPIC QUEST OF DISCOVERY BEYOND WHAT WE CAN SEE

BY JENNA IRVING

Typeset by: Jennifer Toomey

First edition

ISBN 9781738730209

www.jennairving.com

CONTENTS

THE BRAWL

 **1**

THE BRAWL

My heart and mind began to insist in turn,
its usual nocturnal and incessant brawl;
mind, brash and merciless, would not learn,
all fear morphed into a governing law.

Tossing, turning in dubious mental ploys,
taken years and miles far offshore;
I covered my ears to shield the noise,
still being tormented by the bellowing roar.

My tears felt raw and cold they seeped,
I swam in waves with all my strength;
until I drifted off to an aching sleep,
lost after an effort of great length.

My exhausted mind could not cohere,
nor my wearied and sorrowful soul;
taken captive by the terror of fear,
my vision had grown dreadfully dull.

THE DEN

 **2**

THE DEN

When my eyes finally became reflective,
I found myself alone, doomed in a den;
by a mental massive force collective,
of at least one hundred thousand men.

Darkness thick and with dim despair,
no one would covet or pity my stead;
the weight permeating the war-torn air,
bore at least one thousand tons of lead.

I exhaled,

I surveyed,

and in despair,

I relayed:

"Oh! What is life? How do I endure?
To be freed from the agony of fear?
This hard-won earth—I must resist!
Stuck in a foreboding cycle of this sphere.
In the end we tire and suffer alone,
and it does not end—this struggle,
to amass this world, reap what's sown,
while maintaining the mental juggle,
to look brightly at some higher source,
would be a solution to my pain,
only to receive an insoluble silent force,
till I near dub myself insane.
So I remain destitute—a wallowed soul,
destined to be lost, left without control."

Silence prodded and pervaded,
and so did my incendiary sorrow;
all but joy had long invaded,
Oh! To cease thought of
            another tomorrow!

And suddenly, in the slightest periphery,
I caught one glimpse of fragile light;
something pierced my forsaken misery,
on that dark and moonless night:

"Who is this I? This Isolation?
The chime of a small voice, an echo.
I have not felt this much desolation,
since I heard a plea outside Aleppo!

Why do you stay in this somber den,
when clearly you can leave?"

"No way out! I've tried again and again—
what an obvious reason that I grieve!"
I chimed back to the echoing voice,
as if this echo thought I had a choice,

"The peril: it threatens,
the danger: it torments,
no matter where I desperately turn,
my anguish increases—yet never relents."

"Oh, the solution is merely wise!"
the voice stated back with easy mirth.
"You simply open your swollen eyes,
and understand existence on this earth."

What was this sarcastic mock?
A joke of dark hilarity?
I was not he, and he not of my stock,
no existence of self-same clarity.

Easy for this mocking survey—
safe, attuned on the walls outside;
"My eyes are open!" I didn't need to say,
still stating the words back out of pride.

"Oh no, certainly and sadly not,
your fear has bred the saddest of lies:

You think you are bound to this space,
and must remain where you despise.
But I happened upon this darkened place,
a sad, pitiful place you've surmised,
and found the reason you sit without light:

The lumen in your heart has faded.

You've turned a glorious and luminous night,
into this shadowed den you've degraded.
Subconsciously you've chosen to live
in an abode fit for roaming dragons,
your mind accumulating muck like a sieve.

Clear off these visions, these anti-paragons,
own your mind-induced culpability,
and understand your greater capability.
Allow your soul to joyfully emerge,
and understand your greater capacity.

Eradicate the dissonant noise to purge,
and rid yourself of your instability.
Take One deep and profound breath,
until your lungs are strong and full.
Breathe.   And free yourself of death,
Allow yourself to feel the Divine pull.
Do you see?   Do you know?
The world around you? The beauty.
The Wonder. How it glistens just so?
Can you see? It's outside of your 'Me.'
the Divine lives inside: in *Huwa Hu*

—It's merely outside of this *you*.

So uncover your innate, luminous light!
Step out of this cacophonous den,
for then you'll cease this tireless fight,
freed from the mental collective of all men."

My mind listened, eagerly heard,
but I was filled with too much pain;
my soul could recognize the words,
but nothing my mind could obtain.

And so I replied:

"You make it sound like a simple glitch,
but this muck runs deep in years;
it's not a turn of an illumined switch,
that will absorb all of these tears,
my anguish is a force far too great,
and I cannot bear it all so,
I cannot face this mental state,
there's simply no high beyond this low.

So easy on the outside:

You've seen,
You've heard,
You've done.

I've no proof of what you speak of—
Of hope,   I have none.

I'm worn.

I'm beat.

And my will has long since faded.
There's no use in again trying—

For I tried.

I really did."

Silence rang for a long moment,
I thought the voice was gone;
darkness grew around my torment,
mocked by the far away hours of dawn.

**"You're full of foolishness
while you close your eyes.
You must stop riddling your stress.
Do you not actually realize?
The arrows that deliberately hit you?
They're directed from your own bow.
I see clearly what you've been through,
but it's imperative we find your flow.
For there's no way out but up,
and in your pain, you'll find repair.
While the pain that fills your cup,
remains all too much to bear,
a metamorphosis will contend,**

and you'll emerge out of this dragon's den.

Your fear shall end soon!
Just bear the burden of this pain,
for this is your glorious cocoon.
Endure through this inflamed terrain
and you'll emerge
brighter than the fullest moon.
Even if your worst fear insists,
and earth becomes your hell,
your soul is always far from this,

For:

All, is always well.

Like a plane above the clouds and sea,
the earth remains far, far below.
Your problems are not your reality,
but merely all you now know.

Whatever will, whatever was,
is nothing and you know it.
Every action has a cause:

So choose wisely what you emit.

Something clings inside of you,
an energy that feeds on fears.
Each thought, it clouds the view,
ensuring your mind never clears.
Fear it uses as conniving bait,
through every dark thought it's fed.
Because your thoughts cloud your mind
you can no longer see clearly—
while your mind clouds your life,
as you to live in constant strife.

You believe your dreadful thoughts,
and your thoughts make you fear,
you live a life based on *what if*—
afraid you'll lose all you hold dear.

Stop this inner fight and sway,
believe me, there's more than this,
please rest your fear-filled mind—

IT'S ALL GOING TO BE OKAY!"

—

"I appreciate your sincere directive,
but I've already too many times tried;
I'm simply forever fear's captive,
doomed and destined for the dark side.

I've tried to unchain this identity,
but I always end up unwilfully here;
I've tried all advice and every remedy,
but always regress back to fear."

**"Listen, I see you've lost the key,
you've made the efforts that you could.
But, Oh! If only you could see,
what is in store is only infinite good.
I've been sent from deep within,
sent to help revive your soul,
I guarantee you will be freed therein,
to begin: we'll empty your cup
that fear has filled full.
You're taking the long, hard road,
it is you who chooses your fate,
you can find your Divine abode,
yes, challenges always await,**

BUT: Accept these difficult trials,
beyond your torments and fatigue;
for it is then, freedom will prevail,
your soul unchained from all travail.

But it is your choice!

Let go.

Surrender.

To rid yourself of the anti-you;
it is a path for you to renew.
The only way up and out,
        is onward and through.
Remember, keep pressing onward,
your mind will try hard to fool you,
don't look back or try to fast forward,
and again divide yourself in two.
Be patient, it's a path of discovering,
for in the end we suffer alone,
but it's in the solitude of suffering,
that we enter the great Unknown,
it's there we find the Origin,
the Origin of our source and illumination,
where we rise to heights beyond
our very limited imagination."

———

A tranquil silence as light as air,
replaced the still small voice.
And it was then that I became aware,
that I must silence all the noise.
At that precise and peaceful moment,
I felt its heat in my hand,
a majestic key to free me of torment—
the key that helped me understand.

I proceeded through step by step,
by each small speck of determination,
feeble with newfound strength I crept,
yet I knew I was far from elation.

———

As I proceeded, I felt the breeze,
and right before me I saw:
One thousand emerald cypress trees
one hundred glorious feet tall.

Light surged me out of the shallows,
glistening above and between the trees;
it penetrated their darkened shadows,
and there I dropped to my knees.

I felt calm, and nearly at peace,
and tranquil but for a moment;
Would this bliss only increase?
Had I reached the end of torment?

Was I truly once and for all free?
Of all my mind could endlessly invent?
Was this an absolute beginning—Could it be?
Would my incessant thoughts relent?

Time would finally tell,
if I could be free from this damned fear,
to draw from this Divine well,
until my existence became clear.

THE TEST

THE TEST

Bright above amidst my progress,
the ground was glistening with light;
Oh! After years of dubious darkness,
how could my eyes behold this sight?

And yet: Barely three minutes of ease
had filled me full: I could finally imagine hope;
but, it was then, and then between the trees,
I saw it:

The door.

"Don't open it!"
I heard a voice inside me shout,
**"Enjoy this light, this peaceful wonder,
let it all go right now, discard your doubt,
Go on as you were!**

"What if something comes out of that place?"

A slithering voice said in dismay.
I looked at the bough beside me in disgrace,
and there a small creature lay.

It appeared as a small dragon,
but any a beast it could have been;
small in stature, the origin of agon,
I knew then there was no way I'd win.
I jumped back in surprise to say,
"Get away! This is trickery!
this has to be my mind astray,
must I always resort back to this insanity?

"Oh yes, I'm here to protect you,
open this door before it's too late,
ignore that elusive echoing coup
for it doesn't understand
          the safety of your fate,
how can you enjoy this beauty
when there's thoughts you need to quell?
you cannot at all think clearly
until on your problems you dwell,

to ensure everything is alright:
concentrate, ponder, ruminate,
you may have missed a potential plight,
for your safety, you mustn't hesitate!"

Who was this dark voice?
Why must I be tested so soon?
Could I not have a break from this noise?
Was I destined only for absolute ruin?

I stood there in somber contemplation,
remembering the message of the voice;
"Do not open the door to the den."
But did I actually have a choice?

"Enough! You're the divide—
This is only the me and the I!
There's a soul somewhere inside,
Oh! Why must I always comply?"

Before I knew to implore,
fear took all cerebral control,
I opened the darkened door,
felt my mind take over my soul;
captured by fear's hissing spell,
I tumbled down an awful abyss;
down the dark hole I fell,
had I not yet learned to prevent this?
The regression took over me,
as I groped around for the key.

"Stop! Please follow not this disguise!"
I heard a small voice shout.
Do not believe these intrusive lies.
Give not into doom and doubt
that connives to convince your ear,
it's a disguise, merely a ruse!
Allow not the flow of fear,
to rob you of the choice to choose!"

It was then that my mind remembered,
what gave way to hope and wonder;
in fair and golden light—my soul to render,
down I bowed, in humility and surrender.

Words funneled up unaware,
as if summoned by my soul;
some would call it a prayer,
if it so—then I prayed till I felt full:

**"There's never been a wilder will,
than the one that resides within my soul.
Separate from this teeming anguish still,
I know I must relinquish all control.
Guide me on the seeker's flight,
where the Found is always found.
Mercy is at its highest height,
when silence has surpassed all sound.
There's a mercy wilder in revival,
where good things are wrought.
Patience is my pained bitter rival,
Oh! May the seeker be Sought!
The first to seek is often weak,
but stronger shall they grow,
till all is lost in alchemy,
and we surrender all we know."**

I burgeoned out of the harrowing hole,
and back amongst the cypress trees;
I took back my mental control,
and got up off my tear-soaked knees.

I heard that slithering beast
hiss away in hurried flight,
its sour sounds had ceased,

I looked around to see why:

I was covered by an emerald light.

THE FIRE

THE FIRE

Where to go from here but through,
I walked through the marvels of the land;
out of that darkened place I grew,
there was so much now to understand.

All that I thought I ever knew,
was broken down to surrender;
all this clarity I could pursue,
oblivious to this obvious splendor.
Nothing beyond joy could more adorn,
the land different in perspective,
I was out of thought and mind reborn,
freed from the harrowing collective.

Outside of the burgeoning trees,
the mountains lined the horizon;
I began my ascent toward greater heights,
enlivened by the pink skies of the setting sun.

———

It was again I would be tested.
Oh! If I would have been told;
nothing could have suggested,
what was about to unfold.

The edges of the mountain,
became narrow and quite steep;
I began to feel the familiar dread again,
a strong feeling to give up and weep.

I had been soaring in bliss for moment,
but looked off the edge and began to sway;
I looked back ahead to contemplate descent,
but I had already lost my way.
I stumbled, staggered, swayed,
far below me, down the cliff I saw it:

My manifest midnight terror laid,
I was determined not to quit;
but it was far too late—
I could not handle the
      burden of its weight.

Its raging eyes — a bulging abyss,
sending terror straight to my heart;
right then I lost all peace and bliss,
the dragon was far too smart.
I don't know what happened,
or how fast it all unfurled;
but it blew its crimson-blue fire,
and down a spiral I was hurled.

And like in my dreaded dreams,
I found myself spiraling, falling,
down a fastward hopeless tunnel,
while my mind begun foreboding.

———

After falling I landed brusquely,
on the cold midnight ground;
I could see the beast fast behind me,
like a fast-hunting hound.

I may have laid there one hundred years,
or a merely a few short hours;
too hard to tell in the hell I laid,
my soul caught between the bowers.

Any defense or attempt at escape,
the dragon enraged its vociferous fire;
I felt trapped—I felt hopeless,
tangled, knotted in my mental mire.

And finally, that echoing voice—I heard it!
In calm tones it spoke to me,
I passed through my pain as I listened,
and surrendered control in a plea:

**"I know of the dragon that ails you,
how it creeps and disturbs in the night.
Leaving you devastated, panic-stricken,
stuck and submerged in absolute fright.
Your chest narrows and tightens,
your heart constricts and contracts,
Oh! If only you really knew!
This raging dragon is an expression,
of everything but the Divine facts.**

It will continue to return,
as long as you feed your fear,
so look up, not backward or forward.
Discipline fiercely your wily mind:
and your path will be made clear."

I got up onto my feet once more,
exhausted — longing to see the light;
I snuck past as it slept beside me,
feeling the raging fear of my flight.

If he knew I was again trying to escape,
he would end me here and now;
but I focused my attention on the path,
with as much strength as my will
            would allow.
Finally I reached the cliff where I had fallen,
And so I grasped the cold hard rock,
lifting myself back onto the road,
though fear-torn and fragile—
            I began again to walk.

I focused my attention on the path,
not giving face to the strength of fear;
my determination grew stronger,
to not let my thoughts again interfere.

For if I gave power to the thought,
of the dragon when he wakes;
I'd die again in mournful madness,
I could only hope I had what it takes.

THE GUIDE

5

THE GUIDE

Exhausted, I looked for a resting place,
I was nearing the peak of the summit;
weary and fragile I was relieved:
for despite my agony, I had not yet quit.
I narrowed my eyes, and looked ahead,
for far off I could see a figure,
I hoped to hell he was friend not foe,
but my hopes were yet premature.

I sat down in avoidance to not engage,
and mind my own aimless journey;
I laid back against a moss-covered stone,
and began swatting at an angry bee.

"You've engaged yourself in a quarrel,
 I would be still if I were you,
you're only enraging that bee further,
—look what you've gotten yourself into."

The bee was in a frenzied fight,
and bent on his revenge mid-air;
I watched as the man held out his hand,
upon it the bee landed without a care.

He got up close to it and whispered,
what I'll never know;
it then flew off in an upward direction,
and then zoomed off far below.

I looked up at this odd man,
dressed in a humble garb he appeared;
his presence was most surprising,
but nothing alarming to be feared.

"Greetings fellow soul,"
the deep voice resounded.
there was something special about his air
that left my mind confounded.

"Are you ready?" he asked blankly,
his voice was steady in tone.

Who was he talking to? I looked around me,
surely on this mountain we were alone.

His kind eyes gazed at the birds,
his perception was an absolute art;
he communicated not with words,
but from the depths of his heart:

"What is it, O Soul?
What troubles you with such force?
Why do you sit and suffer so?
Are you not aware of a Higher Source?
Or have earthly illusions brought you low?"

"I don't really believe in a 'source.'
for I've sincerely suffered.
I've really suffered.
I don't know what's truth or illusion,
my desperate pleas have yet to be heard."

"How would you know?
You've filled yourself to the brim
with fear and absolute fright.
How do you expect your cup to be filled,
when you've left no room for light?
Begging the heavens to take your suffering,
yet you know nothing of surrender.
You're bent on figuring it out yourself,
this is reason you continue to suffer."

"It's not true! I've sought every solution.
I've begged for the highest mercy;
with tears I've made my ablution,
if a God exists, he's surely forsaken me:
Each night the dragon, it slays me,
where is my heaven-sent help? My aid?
If your God is all powerful, as you decree,
why does he watch idly as I'm slayed?

I'm dead,

I'm done,

Fear has stripped me of all hope,
I'm tired of the endless struggle;
why doesn't your 'God' lend me a rope?
why must I battle this dreaded trouble,
lie in misery on end?
Why does he leave me in sorrow?
Why is no help ever sent?"

**"I'll say it once more, but I see,
you are not yet ready for this door:**

**Begging the heavens to take your suffering,
yet you know nothing of surrender.
You're bent on figuring it out yourself,
this is the reason you continue to suffer."**

With that the lights went out,
only echoing silence remained;
all I've been through, all the doubt,
and here I was, nothing gained.

Then a flickering light enveloped me,
and the guide sat down at my side;
tucking the garb under his feet declared:

"For you, the tools I'll provide:

You are going to pierce this illusion,
for at least 10,000 veils shield your eyes,
from seeing the Truth in its truest profusion:
Trust my words and from the
        ashes you will rise.

Pierce you will, and pierce you shall,
and you'll shatter it from within,
this illusion you battle—this carnival:
Threatens all women and men.
So do not again crumble: Stand tall;
you're about to break the barrier,
where ten thousand veils will fall.

You'll soon surge and soar through the air
to a life you've never once dreamt here,
surpass this all, and you shall in prayer,
—while right now you feel the fire of fear,
You'll soon rise permanently out of despair.

Let's start with the basics, you and me,
and go back to the very beginning.
Much has gotten lost amidst all debris,
since this beautiful earth started spinning."

THE ORIGIN

THE ORIGIN

"Allow me to tell you a simple story,
before the age of the great upheaval,
a story of us, in all Divine glory—
before we understood the concept of evil.
I give you a primordial tale,
before the initial spark of vanity,
this begins your great unveiling,
about our directive—the Purpose of humanity.
Do not forget so easily the sublime,
for this is not our final destination,
we are on earth for a brief time,
then we are absorbed back
            into the Emanation:
This is no matter taken in levity,
so be mindful of life's inherent brevity:

We stood before the Source of All,
in every light of our celestial station,
each soul of us before the fall,
we stood as one at the beginning of creation.
Before the story you know—how it began,
of the First Man and the serpent's tale,
where we were one with the Divine Plan,
before we were known to erroneously fail.
We were high in a heavenly view,
where only the Divine we knew,
there was nothing we wanted more
there was only: *Huwa Hu*.

We were asked by our Origin,
given a question and a test:
Could we be earth's truest viceroys?
Could we maintain loyalty in our quest?
The purpose of your quest of heart,
is to sharpen every faculty,
to realize our great capability,
and unleash the limits of our capacity.
For we are the truest Divine reflection,
if it is only Divine attributes we chose,
for it is only when we chose the opposite:
        it is only then we lose.

Difficult it would be indeed in trust,
to remember the One as we fight,
against the duplicity that tries to fool us,
remaining a true reflection of the Light.

For amidst our mired lives in imbalance,
we might forget the purity of our light;
and become reflections of its absence,
and lose sight of our Divine essence.

For the earth contains rotting roots,
with all-consuming tricks and lies.
If rooted in the depths of evil's attributes,
we are capable of severing Divine ties.

'How could we forget our Origin?'
We asked in shocked surprise.
'There's nothing that could distract us,
from you, The Most Wise!'

'Easy to think as you are innocent,
as you stand before the Light;
but on earth it will be different,
you might struggle to maintain your sight.

Go! And be My true reflections.
My attributes are inherently yours.
Be my extensions, my emanations,
Stay on the straight path, and
        avoid all detours.

Free will you have, and go you may,
a test for those who can reflect,
only for a glimpse, until the Last Day.
If you make a mistake—
        in mercy, I'll correct.'

So we agreed in unison,
to the covenant we made.
To reflect our Divine capacity,
not knowing the meaning
        of being afraid.

So to the task we went in sight,
all surety confident inside us.
We came down from our dewy light,
and on earth acquired the dust.

—

Each thought and will bent,
accumulated slowly on the earth.
This gave rise to the dark moment:

The word "I": the Ego and its birth.

From one to many related,
the veils one by one increased.
Rapidly they accumulated,
blind—our ego became unleashed.

We separated from our inherent Divinity,
from the union with the Divine.
Each one of us became two in entity,
trapped within space and time.

The 'We' turned upside down,
and all faces turned inwards.
After repeatedly crying 'Me'
we all began to see backwards.

Our souls disconnected from their essence,
once filled with only Divinity.
We became attributes of darkness,
unable to distinguish fear from Reality.

What happened next was most grave,
we fell high from our grand elation,
and on earth we muddled it all—
And so, the origin of your misery:
lies in the Great Separation.

So why were we sent here,
knowing we could fail?
The point is not a test of fear,
but the lesson of the tale.

The earth is but a glimpse,
for one day you will see:
You are given a Divine glance,
of our soul's immensity.

More importantly, we realize our privilege,
to be carriers of the Glorious Light.
If we surrender, submit—without sacrilege,
we'll have no problems with our sight.

You see, many years have been passing,
our direct Divine link has long faded.
All that's left, remains a faint longing:
Our minds having long been invaded.

The earth is only but a dream,
not our true destined utopia.
Our souls still rest with the Divine unseen.
Here—we are merely veiled by the
      great myopia."

THE CAPACITY

THE CAPACITY

With these words he then departed,
saying he'd be back in a moment;
so I got up with my heart guarded,
and began exploring the summit.

I walked on in meadowed silence,
lost deep in contemplation;
his words were at a quarrel within me,
yet I felt I needed more explanation.

If I was consumed by this "ego,"
then what was my soul?
Without my thoughts or ideas,
would I not be dreadfully dull?

I sat down under a large oak tree,
and rested my head in my hands;
I then stared up in wonder to see,
hoping I could fully understand.

That all this hope and Divinity,
was real, and not my fear;
I just wanted a key to free me,
so that everything could be clear.

I recognized the truth he spoke,
but still felt the veil of terror;
I knew there must be a way,
to perceive existence without error.

What he spoke of made so much sense,
but my mind remained locked in fright;
I just wanted my lasting freedom!
But I had no strength left to fight.

But oh! I was still strongly veiled,
for it was coming yet again—
the lock on the door had failed,
the damn dragon again prevailed.

I felt its evil gaze summoning,
and the panic rose inside me;
boiled, brewed, and plummeting,
the terror filled me with anxiety.

This time I was consumed quickly,
by the fire it swiftly blew;
enraged, he wished to triumph,
his incendiary hell would surely ensue.

And then, I felt its breath:
the fuel to the devil's empire;
exhausted, I did not fight its death,
so it engulfed me in its fire.

He blew a few more times,
seeing I was not provoked by its rage;
so he picked me up with his teeth,
and placed me in a shadowed cage.

Each day he'd try again,
to rouse me with his fire;
but I just remained there, still—
thinking the guide had been a liar.

"Damn you! Damn you!"
I yelled out at the guide who called himself my aid;
"You've forsaken me, and left me—
Damn you! You sit and watch
             while to death I fade."

And then one moment in anger,
the dragon knocked me over;
and my cage fell with a crash,

And then I watched:

As I dissolved into flecks of black ash.

I drifted without torment,
floating up into the darkness;
and it was at this moment,
that I began to feel my lightness.

I flew up and higher still,
in lightness my body soared;
and then a soft rain began to fall,
and I felt my body restored.

I realized what had just happened,
I had relinquished my greatest contender;
I had simply taken the guide's advice,
and allowed myself to fully surrender.

The moon held high overhead,
and the night glistened with stars;
I knew what must remain unsaid,
It was time to heal these scars.

I woke.
in a cloud of dust, but I woke;
curled up by a fire—a comforting fire,
and then that clear voice spoke.

———

**"You've been through hell, and back again,
it has broken my heart to see it.
But weakness becomes your strength,
when you choose persistence bit by bit.**

**If I help you every time you fall,
you'll never know what to do.
I want to help, and obliterate this wall,
but the only one who can help yourself**

— is you.

You've been given a soul in full trust,
pure, holy, and full of illumined light,
but you've identified with this dust,
bathing yourself in absolute fright."

"You. I thought you abandoned me,
I said as I recalled my shame;
I faulted you, I'm truly sorry,
it's just so hard to play this game."

"I know,
I see what you are going though,
but as long as you empower your fear,
it will have this power over you."

"The feat feels far above me,
I feel poisoned from within;
Every time I think I'm again free,
the dragon emerges out of that den."

"Listen, it's a difficult discipline,
but you simply do not engage.
If you feed your worst fears,
the dragon will surely enrage.

Each time you give a thought attention,
you pull back that bow.
If you feed every *what if*,
you'll shoot every painful arrow.

You then fill yourself with fissures,
where other fears leak through.
Until your veins vibrate so low,
that the collective thinks through you.

So what do you do now, you ask?
It's true–it's no easy feat.
Discipline will be your greatest friend,
if you persevere —
your fear will eventually retreat.

Until one day it fades away,
as a long distant souvenir,
and underneath your atonement,
everything will be made clear.

So when a thought arises,
do not push it away in distraction,
but rise to a higher place,
and force it to lose its traction.

Fear will accompany the harrowing thought,
as an observer watch it pass through.
Do not in a web become again caught,
or it will take full advantage of you.

For your mind tries to protect you,
but has become faulty at best.
It sees everything as an obstacle,
hosting fear as its constant guest.

For fear has cleverly disguised itself,
as your utmost and greatest protector,
but Oh! If only you truly knew,
your fear is only a demonic spectre.

So disarm it with your disciplining,
there is only One who truly protects you.
Trust fully with your entire being,

Breathe:

The only way up, is through.

Watch as your fear bows down,
to the True Power above it all.
Watch as fear hands over its crown,
in the end you'll see it had no power at all.

I know at times you wish to flee,
to escape your misery here,
but that would surely be a dire choice,
for you would shatter the Divine mirror.

I know it's hard to push through this,
but you must accept life's mystery.
All will ultimately be well—with bliss,
so please: embrace life's uncertainty.

Reframe your mind each day,
living not in constant catastrophe.
Everything is going to be okay,
deep inside, you are already free.

But once you have realized,
perhaps the most important lesson to render,
the solution to every plight:
you merely need to

Surrender:

To the Source above it all,
release it all,
and watch your joy increase.

Come, let's finish what I owe,
And please sit down beside me.
Listen, as I give what I know,
let my words guide you till you're free.

Let's begin again at the beginning,
maybe you think there's no
      Power to protect you,
you feel punished and abandoned,
that no one can guide you through.

The veils that shield you from above,
from the Highest Source of All,
are created from cunning lies:

'He's a tyrant.' 'He let me suffer.'
'He's left me to my demise.'

But all veils are false, clouds unaware,
know the truth has long been lost.
Deep inside of you the truth is there,
you've simply chosen the self as the cost."

THE DIVINE

8

THE DIVINE

"Let's begin with the term worship,
let's tear all the veils away.
It's not the notion we think of:
it's defined another way.

It's not the prostration before idols,
or the burning on an altar,
not a life of sequestered silence,
or some pilgrimage afar,
it is a carrying,
a reflection,
of the attributes Divine,
a paragon of worship:
a mirror of at least one of ninety-nine.

To carry Divine attributes,
both an honor yours and Above,
for this is how you mold as One,
true worship is a reflection of love.

You mirror the Divine reflection,
if you carry love, you carry Divinity,
generosity, kindness—all virtues,
is attaining Divine proximity.

You see, if you carry fear,
do you know whose attribute it belongs?
The ego who originates all error:
the mischief-maker of all wrongs.

See, if you were careful,
you would choose wisely what to reflect.
For surely if only you knew,
that all the negativity you feel,
is where the devil and ego intersect.

I've seen men throw away their hearts,
and trade them for a disguise.
A mask that triumphs all authenticity,
while they masquerade themselves as wise.

You this, you that, they soak God
        or others with all blame.
Anything to point their finger
away from their cunning masquerades,
as they reflect nothing in the mirror.

Heaven forbid they drop all hate,
and choose love within instead.
But all's been lost to ego lust,
inside their heart is dead.

They've twisted prophets' words into a knot,
and spit a spell upon it.
In their perception they've funneled poison,
and hate for they know not what.

What is man if he hates another?
Why is it not love he chooses?
If his ego is fully saturated,
he cannot see it is love he loses.

It is sorrowful and sad what has been,
that we cling not together to the rope.
But to the self we worship within—
as man loses love, he also loses hope.

Here I remind of the possibility,
that all were one—one we are all.
Deeply we hold this inherent unity,
for we are all from a bursted star.

As our light spread in flecks,
we each fell to our own place,
becoming enamored with the earth,
forgetting the reflection of our Divine face.

Oh if only we could have predicted,
the devils and their egoic snare,
they forgot the One and blamed Him quickly,
in the name of 'justice,'
          they decided what was fair.

So decide, which are you?
Someone who loves or blames.
Do you forgive?
Or give heat to the devil's flames?

Here's how to tell,
if your mind has bred more lies:
Do you feel the terror of fear?
Then yes—whatever it is—is trying
to lead you to your demise.

So know well who you are,
for you are not fear's pawn.
You are not meant for illusion,
for you come from the light
            that breaks at dawn.

You are a mirror and a reflection,
meant to emanate the Divine.
You are an endless ocean,
—outside of space and time.

You are filled with a Power,
to banish all of evil's attributes.
If you feel something negative,
then willfully tear out the roots.

And start again with surrender,
give power to your Divine reflection.
Know that you are separate from fear,
but one with the mirror of
            Divine projection.

Rely only on the One,
and not on your fear.
For fear will only create more sorrow,
of forever losing all you hold dear,
while you live in an endless tomorrow.

There's absolutely nothing on this earth,
that you should give any importance.
Except for love and your Divine mirror,
everything else is a transitory insignificance.

Let it go.

Be free.

Rest and be assured.

All the worry plaguing you,
will all soon in turn pass:
For anything of the earth,
will return to dust and ash.

Take your time but do not hesitate,
and give not up or accept defeat.
Travel but don't let your mind dictate,
stop not till you reach where
        the two seas meet.

Even if it takes your whole life,
make sure you reach this place.
(and bring the fish)
Make good use of all this strife,
this is where the self-will efface.

You will know what to do,
it's not easy but now is the time.
To free yourself of this *you*,
onward you'll go, up and through.
The juncture you will know,
He'll be standing there, the Green Guide.
Man in emerald—soul as pure as snow,
you'll see the rock, with the low tide.

Once you let go of earthly form,
and your self-created dystopia,
you will perceive without veils,
and be freed of the great myopia."

THE CHOICE

9

THE CHOICE

With that I went out and walked the coast,
knowing it was time to release what bled;
though painful it was, what I needed most:
Release the mind and let the heart rule instead.

I traveled far and wide to find this place,
the juncture where the two seas meet;
I knew this guide would be the face,
to show me how to rise above defeat.

I thought I arrived at the juncture,
but realized I had forgotten the fish!
So I had to dissuade my hunger,
and proceed with my soul's wish.

I waited until the sun was low,
just about 7 o'clock;
and there he was, he knew me,
he was kneeling on the rock.

He didn't speak but motioned,
his hand illumined by green light;
looked at me and approached,
then turned to face the night.

Seas in a great expanse before us,
I watched as he kneeled and took some sand;
saying a prayer, he grasped the dust:
I watched as he threw out his hand:

**"Take the dust you've created,
and toss it far out to sea.
Take the dust you've accumulated,
and unlimit your capacity.**

**The choice is yours to make,
to live solely for you or for—
(he pointed his finger upwards)
Once you rid yourself of this "I"
you'll never return again as before.**

Your life will change miraculously,
you will see with a golden light.
Everything you ever thought of life,
will be recalibrated and set right.

Be careful how you choose,
for life is a sum of choices.
Life is meant to be lived in full,
freed is the one who rejoices!

So take the dust you're filled with,
and throw it out to sea.
Take the dust you're consumed with,
and unleash your immensity.

Let go of the me, the I, and the mine,
You're done with all of this.
You can only access the high Divine,
when freed from the self-entwined.

So take the dust you're veiled with,
and surrender it to the seas.
Take the dust that covers your vision,
and unveil infinite possibilities.

With that he became silent,
and the breezy air became a cover;
the night quieted with his stillness,
as the stars began to hover.

I stood there on the brink of choice,
to empty once and for all for good;
I watched the sea, still hearing his voice,
planting my feet where I stood.

Echoing:

Take the dust that veils you,
and surrender it to the sea.
Purify yourself of the "me"
and allow the real You to be.

I bent and took a handful of sand,
and made a pledge for my freedom;
I looked over at the Green Guide's hand,
One finger pointing upward—above.

Outside the confines of "I"
I could live in an Infinite Space;
earth would be my paradise,
in my heart I could live with grace.

The idea of 'me' since birth,
the self I had unknowingly instated;
through many years on earth,
living finite while the Infinite awaited.

It isn't a task or a lesson,
or even a solution to render;
the key out of every dark den,
is simply the practice of:

SURRENDER.

So I will my soul to joyfully emerge,
and understand my greater capacity;
the noise is all that's left to purge,
and realize my innate sagacity.

It is now that I can finally see:

The Divine lives inside,

But outside of this "me."

The dust of the self grows,
acquired with each use of 'I'
—Each thought is merely:
A choice of truth or lie.

And I realized all this time,
I had grappled with Divine existence;

But it wasn't the Divine to be questioned:

—But the false existence of *mine*.

The dust of the false me,
the separation from Divine;
to enter the state of living,
free from the self-entwined.

To leave the lands of self-induced dystopia,
and finally—Be freed of the great myopia.

So I took the dust within me,
and tossed it out to sea,
and realized once and for all:

This was the clearest way to see.

ABOUT THE AUTHOR

Jenna Irving studied English at the University of Victoria. The Great Myopia is her first work of published poetry. She currently resides in British Columbia.

You can find her at www.jennairving.com.

Milton Keynes UK
Ingram Content Group UK Ltd.
UKHW021307310823
427834UK00025B/702